THE
Archive Photographs
SERIES

BARNSLEY

Artist's impression of the south west view of Barnsley from Far Well Field in the early 1800's.

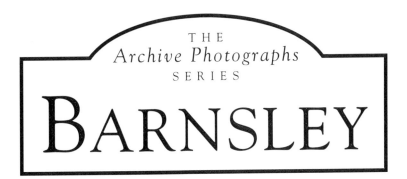

THE
Archive Photographs
SERIES

BARNSLEY

Compiled by
Barnsley Archive Service

CHALFORD

First published 1995
Copyright © Barnsley Archive Service, 1995

The Chalford Publishing Company
St Mary's Mill, Chalford,
Stroud, Gloucestershire, GL6 8NX

ISBN 0 7524 0188 2

Typesetting and origination by
The Chalford Publishing Company
Printed in Great Britain by
Redwood Books, Trowbridge

Contents

A lone boy posing on Shaw Lane Pumps, still in use as a water supply until the early 1900's.

Introduction

The contemporary view of Barnsley is of an industrial town with little or no roots other than coal. However many would be surprised to learn that Barnsley's heritage travels much further back into the abyss of time.

Barnsley was initially a market town which served the farms and villages throughout the surrounding area. This fact is not surprising when one considers the reputation Barnsley Market holds today. By the middle of the seventeenth century, while still only small in population, the town was thriving. This was especially due to its ideal geographical position, situated between Wakefield and Sheffield, and an ideal resting point for travellers crossing the Pennines.

With these advantages we can clearly see however, why Barnsley was to become so prominent during the Industrial Revolution in the nineteenth century. Such topographical advantages and ready economic facilities were always going to be the beginnings of a dynamic industrial town.

The Linen Industry developed first and so often in people's minds it takes second place to the coal mining industry. However, it is evidence enough to quote *Slater's Directory* of 1848 which stated that 'in Barnsley the manufacture of linen goods of every description preponderates, many thousands of looms being employed in the town and in adjacent villages'. In 1850 there were about 3000 handloom weavers in the town alone. In addition there were steam looms, introduced in 1837, and by the 1850s a cluster of linen mills had emerged in the Town End area, drawing water from the Sough Dike to feed their millponds. By 1871, one of these mills, Taylors in Peel Street, was described in a trade directory as 'the biggest mill of its kind in the country'. By 1880, this mill housed over 400 steam looms and employed over 800 people.

The industry, however, was in decline because, by the end of the century, competition from Scotland and Ireland in the 1860s and 1870s had undermined the confidence of management and discouraged investment. Needless to say, the downfall of the linen industry did not dampen the enthusiasm of the Barnsley population as they had another trade to turn to, from which they could make their living – mining.

There was a considerable amount of coal beneath Barnsley. It was enough not only to supply the Town's needs, but to export to other industrial communities thirsty for the fuel of the Industrial Revolution. By the middle of the nineteenth century the advent of coal in Barnsley had caused the creation of an intricate transport network to cope with the export demands. The canal was extended to Barnsley so that the coal could be transported to Hull and Goole; the opening of the South Yorkshire and Great Northern Railway in the early 1850's also had a great effect on the mining economy. As far as the effects on Barnsley were concerned from the 1850's onwards coal became the most important industry in Barnsley and by far the largest employer.

The economic boom brought by mining was to continue well into the twentieth century and Barnsley could easily boast that it was the principal coal town in South Yorkshire. The evidence of this success is obvious to all who look around the area even now. The villages which expanded, for example Grimethorpe and Dodworth are the epitome of the typical mining village. Many social activities, brass bands and mining unions were binding features of these new communities.

One must not however forget the many lives that were lost during this era. The explosion at Swaithe Main Colliery, on 6 December 1875, saw the loss of 145 lives. Barnsley's worst mining disaster was the Oaks Colliery explosion in which 350 men and boys were killed. One must also consider the conditions in which these men worked. Considered modern in their day, the working conditions were however extremely cramped and dangerous. It is easy to understand why the Miners' Permanent Relief Fund was so popular.

Sadly, for the people of Barnsley the mining industry went into decline in the 1960s. The town, however, has managed to put on a brave face and has resorted to its first niche in life – as a market town. Over the past thirty years Barnsley town centre has been completely modernised. The new market and the Alhambra Shopping Centre attract visitors to Barnsley from all round the area. Barnsley has reverted to its roots as a thriving market town.

Our main aim in the creation of this book, while showing a brief picture of Barnsley's heritage, is to show the changes which Barnsley has undergone, even within the small time in our history in which photography has been available. The structural changes of the landscape have been immense. The photographic images of these changes give an insight into the activities and lives of the Barnsley people and the upheavals they have surmounted. Many people will recognise the streets, buildings and faces within the book while for others it may come as a surprise to see how Barnsley once looked.

If anyone, after reading this book, wishes to look at any of the photographs or to study any of the institutions, all relevant material is available for viewing at the Barnsley Archive Service, Central Library, Shambles Street, Barnsley. We welcome any questions concerned with the documented history of the area and look forward to hearing from you.

Miss Louise Whitworth (Archivist),
Barnsley Archive Service.

One

Barnsley
Past and Present

MARKET HILL, BARNSLEY. 19.

The cobbled Market Hill between the Wars. Note that Whitelams, Maudslay and Krakuer are no more, but are the site of the new Town Hall.

The entrance to the Arcade from Market Hill, probably in the first decade of the 1900's. The photograph features the shops, from left to right, Butterfields, Hirst's and Guest's.

10

Church Street (formerly known as Kirkgate), post 1923. To the left of the photograph can be seen Arthur Wright's Dispensing Chemist, which was established in 1923. Also note the Royal Hotel, which began its life known only as the 'Royal', being a coaching inn from where the mail left for London.

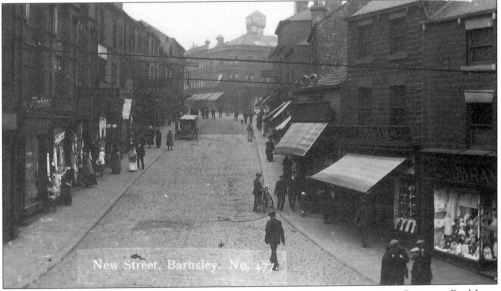

New Street, looking up towards the Barnsley British Co-operative Society Building, 1927–1930. B. Ouram established his Baby Linen Shop in 1867, to be followed by George Ouram opening his Hosiery Shop, next door in 1899. Also, note the large pair of spectacles over R.E. Gray's shop, the optician from 1898–1927.

The changing face of Town End. Town End looking up towards Peggy Mill, taken before 1889.

Town End sees the invention of traffic lights. In the centre of the photograph you can see the Wheatsheaf pub, situated between Dodworth Road and Racecommon Road. There was a long dispute to stop the closure of this pub. However, eventually it was demolished to make way for the Western Relief Road Scheme.

Town End, September 1990, during the construction of the Western Relief Road.

Market Day, outside the Wellington Hotel, May Day Green. The Wellington Hotel replaced the Lamb Inn in 1868, and was pulled down in 1967.

Shoe shining on the cobbled streets of May Day Green, *c.* 1880–1890's.

Men working on the tram lines in May Day Green. See how the crowds gathered to watch this event *c.* 1880–1890's.

Queen Street, 1911–1929. Shops of interest are the Maypole Dairy Company, seen on the right, established in 1911, and the store marked 3/9 was Jackson Limited, the Hatters, established in 1910 and closed in 1929. These shops were to become the site for Woolworths in 1932.

Queen Street again, this time showing a more modern view with shops we are accustomed with today. On the right is Marks and Spencer Limited, this store in Barnsley opened in 1937, and on the left handside of the street, Burton Limited, Tailors, opened in 1930.

Huddersfield Road with a clear view of the obelisk. W C Mence did not take too kindly to travellers knocking on the door of his home and asking directions. His solution was to construct an obelisk as a guide post near his home. It was situated at the junction of Hollowgate (now Victoria Road), Old Mill Lane, Church Street and Church Lane, Note that when it was constructed Huddersfield Road was not in existence. The Obelisk was taken down in 1931.

Wetting the whistle at Kendray Street Fountain. Erected in 1887, the Kendray Fountain was built by the Metropolitan Drinking Fountain Association and cost the patron, Mrs Ann Alderson Lambert about three hundred pounds. The unveiling ceremony was performed by the Mayor Alderman Marsden in April 1887. The fountain was in memory of Mrs Lambert's late father and mother Francis and Ann Kendray.

The Public Hall situated on Eldon Street. The Public Hall was opened in February 1878, by the Mayor of Barnsley, who was accompanied by the Mayor of Pontefract, Mr Alderman Phillips, the Mayor of Rotherham, Mr Alderman Morgan and the ex-Mayor of Wakefield, Mr Alderman Gill. The inaugural ceremony was a brief affair which consisted merely in the presentation of the Freedom of the Hall in the form of a solid silver key, to the Mayor. He is said to have accepted this key with 'mingled feelings of diffidence and gratitude'.

The tree lined Gawber Road, *c.* 1930's.

Market Day in Barnsley, at the beginning of the century.

May Day Green, showing a view of the Market. In the background is the Cross Keys Hotel, opened in 1825 and closed in 1972. The name, W Barnes above the sign was the name of the landlord, who resided at the Cross Keys Hotel, between 1897 and 1924. Also, notice the tram in the foreground. Trams made a very early appearance in Barnsley Market Place.

The market again, this time, outside Barraclough's Foundry.

16 August 1937. Washday at Oak Street, off Racecommon Road. Notice the family bath hanging on the wall.

18 August 1937, Wall Street, before the Oak Street Clearance Order of 1937. The photograph shows, numbers 2, 4, 6 and 8, Well Street and the entrance to Court 1, Racecommon Road.

A view of New Street and Baker Street prior to the New Street (Eastern) Clearance Order of the 1930's.

The residents of Numbers 4, 6 and 8 Albert Street, 20 August 1937.

Heelis Street in the 1950's, showing a style of Weaver's Cottages. The most impressive building on this street, was the Wesleyan Mission Chapel, built in 1878. The chapel was a plain brick building, accommodating more than 300 people. Under the chapel there was a school room and two classrooms.

Regent Street Congregational Church. The church was formally opened for public worship on 25 September 1856. However, the church was constituted by the Reverend Mark Docker in January 1825 when the Salem Chapel was opened. The Church with school rooms owed its existence mainly to Mr William Shaw of Wakefield, who was a native of Worsbrough Dale and who gave one half of the cost of the building, giving a grant of £500. The remaining portion of money was raised by voluntary offerings of the congregation and friends.

St George's Church, consecrated in 1822. The parish church of St George the martyr was a Waterloo church, built out of a one million pounds parliamentary grant for the building of new churches, as a national thanksgiving for the defeat of Napoleon at Waterloo. Sadly, this impressive building began suffering from structural problems in the 1980's and had to be demolished in October 1993.

Beckett Hospital, established 14 March 1865 and founded by John Staniforth Beckett, with a view to providing efficient drugs and medicines and medical advice for such inhabitants of the town of Barnsley who were incapable by reason of poverty or otherwise to obtain such help.

A view inside the children's ward of Beckett Hospital. The extension to Beckett Hospital to create a children's ward was built in 1900. It was built to provide 18 beds for the special treatment of children.

St Helen's Hospital, c. 1928. Built in 1883, the hospital was then the infirmary portion of the Barnsley Workhouse and was controlled and administered by the Board of Guardians. In 1936, the name Infirmary was changed to St Helen's Hospital, and the hospital continued to provide treatment, mainly of chronic sick patients, a few maternity cases and mental cases.

The demolition of St Helen's Hospital. The hospital was demolished to make way for the new Barnsley District General Hospital, with phase one of the operation starting in 1971. The last part of St Helen's Hospital was demolished in 1976.

Beevor Hall, built in the second half of the eighteenth century by William Jackson. In 1922, the Hall was bought by the Barnsley Brewery Company, and became its administrative offices.

The Barnsley Olympia Ice Skating Rink. It was built in 1909, only to be changed into the Pavilion Cinema in 1920. The building was destroyed by fire in 1950.

The Empire Palace, Westgate, which was better known as the Old Surrey Music Hall and was demolished in 1954. Both George Formby Snr and Marie Lloyd played at the Music Hall.

The Old Tithe Barn in Westgate. The Barn was demolished in 1968.

Queen's Market, Joe Edward's Pot Stall, in the corner by the steps, leading to Eldon Street.

Morning milk delivered on Granville Street, by Harold Pickering.

The Three Cranes Hotel, Queen Street, in the early 1930's. It was built in 1930 and closed in 1963 to make way for a new larger Woolworths.

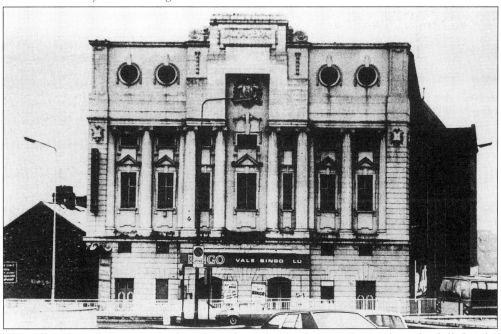

The Alhambra Theatre, opened on Monday 4th October 1915. Heading the bill for the opening week was one of England's favourite artists, Miss Victoria Monks, known as 'John Bull's girl'. In 1921, the Theatre was converted into a cinema, closing in 1960 and later becoming a Bingo Hall. This photograph was taken just before its demolition in 1982. The new Alhambra Shopping Centre was built on this site.

Old Weavers Cottages, called Malton Place at Pitt Street, built in 1860.

The Three Travellers, now known as Draycotts. It is the only public house remaining from the twenty eight which used to be in Shambles Street.

The Cattle Market at Midland Street, *c.* 1930, opened in 1884 to try to encourage business to Barnsley.

Barnsley Open Market, *c.* 1970's. Barnsley received its Market Charter in 1249, and has held regular markets ever since. This photograph was taken just before the new market was built.

Barnsley Bus Station, 1938.

Woolworths on Queen Street *c*. 1971–1973. The photograph shows the original Woolworth's store which was opened in 1932. The building under construction on the left hand side of the photograph is Phase One of the new Woolworth's building which was opened in 1971. The two stores were then incorporated to form one, to be opened in March 1973.

The rebuilding of the Market Complex at Cheapside, July 1972.

The foundation of Barnsley Market as we know it today, July 1972.

448. MARKET HILL BARNSLEY.

Two views of Market Hill. The first looking up towards the Town Hall was taken *c.* 1953–1954.

Looking down Market Hill from the Town Hall on 20 January 1971. Notice the appearance of concrete lamp posts, as opposed to the first view. Market Hill was the first street to obtain concrete lamp posts in Barnsley, in 1954.

A view of Queen Street from Cheapside, prior to pedestrianisation, 1979.

Barnsley's War Memorial erected to commemorate the victims of the First World War. This view was completely changed in 1933, when the new Town Hall was built.

Barnsley Town Hall in the early 1970's. The building is an excellent example of civic architecture for its period and is easily recognised as the work of architects Lancaster and Lodge. Its classical proportions and detailing in Portland stone proudly crown Market Hill and dominate the town.

Two
The Backbone of Barnsley

Annie Christine Fountain, the daughter of Mr Joseph Fountain of Birthwaite Hall, cutting the ground with a silver spade for Woolley Colliery in August 1910. Joseph Fountain was the founder of Woolley Colliery and Annie Christine was the chief share holder in the business. The colliery was one of Barnsley's largest employers, at one stage employing 2000 men. The colliery closed in 1987.

Barnsley Main Oaks Colliery with Great Central Railway wagons standing on the pit sidings. There are three shafts visible.

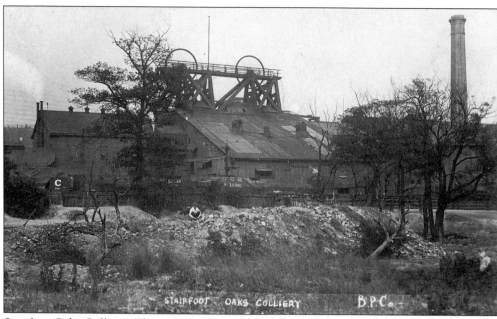

Stairfoot Oaks Colliery. This pit was the scene of one of Britain's worst peacetime disasters since the fire of London. The Oaks explosion of 1866 claimed the lives of over 350 men and boys. Many of the bodies were never recovered.

Pigeon racing was a favourite pastime of miners. Here we have a group of men from Silkstone.

The shift is over! Miners pose for this photograph after a days work in 1909.

Elsecar Main Colliery. Note the two forms of transport, canal and rail. The canal was also used to keep cool on hot days.

Barnsley Main Rescue Team No. 1, 1931. Working underground with such equipment was very uncomfortable and at times very dangerous.

Grimethorpe Pit was sunk into the Barnsley Seam in October 1894. It was the work of the Mitchell Main Colliery Company which already operated two other pits in the area. The first sod of ground for Grimethorpe Colliery was cut by Mr G H Turner, General Manager of the Midland Railway Company. The Colliery was closed in 1993.

Wombwell Main Colliery was sunk in 1853. It had a chequered history. In 1862, the coal ignited and the men had to be encased in diving bell dresses for the subsequent explorations. In 1904, the Parkgate seam was closed and 200 men and boys were laid off. The pit finally closed in 1969.

Direct from coal face to boiler. In boiler house excavations at Barnsley Corporation's Electricity Works in June 1925, a seam of useful coal 1 foot 8 inches thick was discovered. Twenty tons were immediately removed from beneath one of the boilers and coal was fed directly into the stoker, producing several hours of fuel.

Herbert Keeling and Ned the Pony. Ned was the last pony out of Pilley Pit in 1957. Both Herbert and the pony were able to retire together.

Wharncliffe Silkstone Colliery, *c.* 1896. There were five shafts sunk, the first of which was in 1853. In 1914 , an explosion occurred which claimed the lives of 11 men; John Wordsworth, George Bailey, Walter Bailey (father and son), Harry Littlewood, Joseph Siddall, Fred Walker, Oscar Wood, John Fearnley, William Fisher, Henry Gardner and Arthur Norman.

Coke ovens at Wharncliffe Silkstone Colliery in the 1930's. Note the railway wagons which advertise the name of the Company.

Mr Clark (the gentleman wearing glasses), shown here, with his colleagues, in the lamp room at Wharncliffe Silkstone Colliery, c. 1930's.

Screening the coal at Wharncliffe Silkstone Colliery. This was where the coal was sorted and graded.

The joiner's shop at Wharncliffe Silkstone. George Stanley is pictured in the centre of the photograph.

Pit Hill Weigh House at Wharncliffe Silkstone Colliery.

Pit pony wearing the latest in lighting fashion. The lights were made by Ceag, a local Barnsley company who also made safety lights and other electrical devices.

Mitchells Main Colliery was sunk in 1870 and coal was won in 1875. It was an international pit, being under the ownership of an Englishman, Mr Joseph Mitchell and a Frenchman, Mr Josse. The area of the colliery was 450 acres, and it was hoped it would yield 4 million tonnes of coal. The pit closed officially in 1956.

Hoyland Silkstone Colliery was situated six miles south east of Barnsley and opened in 1873. The land was leased by the Hoyland Silkstone Coal and Coking Company Ltd of which Mr T Birch of Manchester was the Chairman. The company had a total of 148 coking ovens attached to the colliery.

Wharncliffe Woodmoor, c. 1916. The pit was situated two and a half miles north of Barnsley at Carlton. The Colliery was sunk between 1874 and 1877, when two shafts were sunk by Mr Joshua Willey. A famous figure of Wharncliffe Woodmoor is Roy Mason, MP for Barnsley, and now in the House of Lords.

A working mine, set in a desolate landscape, *c.* 1980's.

The Colliery at North Gawber was established in 1853.

THE "LATEST" IN HEAD GEAR.
1912 STRIKE, WARREN QUARRY LANE,

The 1912 strike, photographs of two scenes at Warren Quarry Lane, Barnsley. The strike was due to the issue of the minimum wage. The strike caused much distress , and the King refused to leave London until he had seen the Prime Minister, Mr Asquith .

Coal picking. Due to the poverty caused by the 1912 strike, the people of Barnsley had to produce their fuel by any means possible.

Cudworth Miners receiving strike pay in the 1926 strike.

National Union of Mineworkers, Yorkshire Area Headquarters, early 1900's. The building was built in 1874 for the South Yorkshire and Derbyshire Miners Association. Note the two different forms of transport on Victoria Road.

Darfield Main, 1965. Coal was won in 1860. At the time of nationalisation, Mitchells Main at Wombwell was closed and all the employees were transferred to Darfield. Darfield itself was closed in July 1989, after a temporary reprieve in 1985.

Woolley Colliery, 1972. The Wheatley Wood seam at Woolley Colliery was sunk in 1869, followed by shafts numbered 1 and 2 in 1912. Number 3 shaft was sunk in 1942. The pit was closed in 1987.

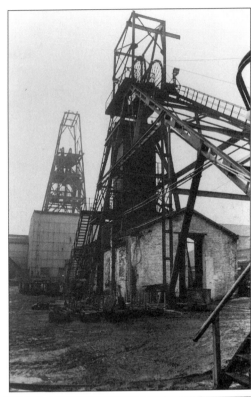

Rockingham Colliery, 1962. The shafts were sunk in 1874 and 1875. The pit closed in 1979.

West Riding Miners Permanent Relief Fund Friendly Society, Board of Management . This fund was set up in 1877, to provide relief and assistance to miners and their families in times of sickness or in the event of a fatal accident. It continued to provide relief right up until 1980, when modern welfare made it unnecessary.

Three
Feasts, Fun and Families

The men of the Rose and Crown, Crane Moor Football Team, surrounded by flat capped supporters.

11 July 1897. At a money raising event held for Gawber Hospital, bowler hats and brollies shelter the crowds from the summer sun.

The County Borough of Barnsley's first aviation meeting took place on Feast Tuesday 1913, at the Court House Station. Mr B C Hucks, one of England's finest airmen, flew the Bleriot in front of a crowd of almost 10,000. He invited spectators to accompany him on his flight, but only Mr C H Cobbold volunteered. He was taken on a 10 minute flight around Barnsley. People lined the streets to watch the ace airman flying through the air at about 3,000 feet.

Dressed in their Sunday Best, the members of Crane Moor's Wesleyan Sunday School and Thurgoland Wesleyan School, join forces for the Whitsuntide Parade through Thurgoland, 1902.

A seaside trip for the people of Staincross and Mapplewell. Getting a suntan was obviously not a priority in the 1930's.

ALE AND CAKE DAY MAUNDY THURSDAY DISCONTINUED

Maundy Thursday was ale and cake day in Penistone in the late 1800's. The popular custom was discontinued in 1905.

The children hold out their bags, as Frank Tinker and Rufus Peace carry out the ancient custom of giving out rye to the poor of Penistone, *c.* 1910.

'Be Prepared'. Goldthorpe Boy Scouts enjoy an afternoon in the great outdoors.

Flags wave, and crowds gather for the opening ceremony of the Town End Recreation Ground,
29 June 1905.

In the shadow of the Star Paper Mill, residents of The Fleets congregated on the frozen
reservoir. Spectators brought their own chairs.

The Salvation Army Band of Barnsley, 1908–9, in all their glory.

The triumphant Royston Silver Band, proudly display the cup won at Crystal Palace in 1921. The band are pictured outside Yardley's Mansion, and later became known as the Monckton Colliery Band.

The Crane Moor and Stainbrough Brass Band in action, *c.* 1900.

The victorious Thurnscoe Harmonic Male Voice Choir. The man proudly holding the cup, is conductor, Ernest Smith. The Choir are pictured here outside Hickleton Hall, 1929.

The Old Surrey Music Hall in Westgate was the last remaining old time theatre in town, and was demolished in February 1955. At various stages in the history of the building, the Surrey was known as the Empire Palace, and in its later days used as premises for the Barnsley West End Working Men's Club. More recently, it was used as a paper warehouse.

Goldthorpe United Football Club team photograph, 1903–4. The Captain of the team, guarding the ball is Mr W Owen.

The hard men of Barnsley Rugby Football Club are pictured here during the 1947–8 season.

The demure young ladies of the Barnsley Life Saving Class, pose for the 1927 team photograph.

The male contingent of the Barnsley Life Saving Class, model the latest fashion in swimwear, 1927.

Battle of the sexes at Elsecar. The Elsecar Ladies' and Gentlemen's Cricket Teams play for victory, *c.* 1910.

World War One equality! Empire Mills Female Football Club, 1917.

Barnsley Football Club victorious English Cup winners, pictured here in 1910.

This stand at Barnsley Football Ground has now been demolished, to make way for the all seater stadium.

THE KING AND QUEEN'S VISIT TO BARNSLEY JULY 10TH 1912

DU-2505

King George V and his wife Queen Mary on their visit to Barnsley, 10 July 1912. Their procession up Market Hill is slowed down by the large number of onlookers who have gathered to welcome the Royal couple.

The King and Queen visit Elsecar Main Colliery, as part of their tour of various industrial sites in Yorkshire. On this occasion 9 July 1912, the King actually travelled down into the pit.

Crowds gather on the rooftops, and fill every available space on Market Hill, to watch King George V receiving the Mayor of Barnsley, 10 July 1912.

The people of New Street, Great Houghton, hold a street party to celebrate the marriage of Princess Margaret and Lord Snowden, 6 May 1960.

The people of Barnsley turn out *en masse* and fill Kendray Street to capacity to cheer the Queen, who was in Barnsley to open the new market, July 1977.

'Long May She Reign'. The Queen on walkabout on a glorious day in July 1977.

The bride looks radiant in this 1920's wedding photograph.

A wedding party photographed at the turn of the century.

The Cudworth branch of the Association of Railway Servants march in the Orphan Fund Procession, on Barnsley Road, 1909.

The courageous ladies of the National Union of Women's Suffragettes, march through the streets of Barnsley, in the hope of gaining converts and publicity for the cause, July 1913.

SPECIAL RECRUITING CAMPAIGN,
BARNSLEY. AUG. 1ST, 1915.

A special recruiting campaign for the war effort was held in the town of Barnsley, 1 August 1915.

GIAN REFUGEES
BARNSLEY 1914

Men, women and children from Belgium who fled the horrors of the First World War, and were given refuge in Barnsley, 1914.

'Welcome Home Boys'. Crowds gather as the brave Barnsley Battalions return home from the war, 29 May 1919.

'War is Over', peace day celebrations in Penistone, 1919.

Crane Moor local defence workers, *c.* 1940.

Men and boys gather outside The Corner Pin, and Imperial Hotel in Peel Square to admire Barnsley's First World War tank, 1 July 1919.

Prime Minister David Lloyd George inspecting the men of the York and Lancaster Regiment on Eldon Street on 27 August 1921. During the Great War, the Regiment won Battle Honours at Ypres, the Somme, Messines, Passchendale, Cambrai, Lys, Selle, Piave, Macedonia and Gallipoli.

Crowds gather as the Prime Minister David Lloyd George and his wife arrive at the wedding of Sir William Sutherland and Annie Christine Fountain at Darton Parish Church on 27 August 1921.

Mr Edward George Lancaster inspecting the proud nurses of Barnsley, possibly during or just after the First World War. Mr Edward George Lancaster was one of Barnsley's most worthy townsmen, and he was the founder of the Church of St Edward, King and Confessor. When built in 1902, for about £3,000, Mr Lancaster was responsible for the whole cost, and through his generosity and donation of £1,500, it was possible for St Edwards to build the Parish Hall in 1931.

'Blessing of the drums', York and Lancaster Regiment take part in the presentation of the King's Colours, Market Hill, 8 April 1923.

The ambulance workers and air raid personnel of Goldthorpe pose proudly, 1939.

Wounded soldiers spent their convalescence potato picking at Lundwood Hospital, April 1917.

The Yorkshire Agricultural Show took place on August 8, 9 and 10th, 1907.

Hoyland Boy Scouts tuck in, 1942.

On Saturday January 11 1908, a terrible tragedy occurred at the Public Hall (now known as the Civic Hall), Barnsley. A fire broke out in the hall, and in the panic that followed, 16 children were killed in the stampede to escape. This postcard was issued to commemorate the children who lost their lives.

King George VI and Queen Elizabeth are greeted by the Mayor and Mayoress of Barnsley during their visit in 1944.

Four
Working Barnsley

Armed with £30, Mr George Kay and a group of like-minded friends purchased a small shop on Market Street. On 13 March 1862, the shop opened its doors to the public and the first branch of the Barnsley British Co-operative Society was born. The remarkable success of the Society was marked with the opening of their Wellington Street and Market Street store in December 1916. This photograph was taken in 1952.

Continued expansion, the laying of the foundation stone for the Yews Lane branch at Worsbrough Dale in 1935.

Where it all began. The first branch of the BBCS pictured here c. 1875.

Hoyland Town branch. The store was one of the first in a period of rapid expansion during 1873.

Another village, another branch. This time Monk Bretton, which was opened in 1877.

Hoyle Mill, fully staffed, c. 1900.

The first branch store of the BBCS was opened in Dodworth on 21 February 1863. The first day's takings were 8s. 3d.

Barnsley Road, Wombwell, which was managed by Mr W Skidmore.

Self -service has arrived. The Washington Avenue Co-op branch, Wombwell, *c.* 1970's.

Redbrook Linen Mill. At one time, one of Barnsley's main industries was the production of linen. By the late 1800's the name of Barnsley Linen was widely known as a product of high quality. In 1869, when Barnsley became a borough, half the coat of arms was devoted to the linen trade. In 1930, Redbrook Linen Mill was honoured by receiving orders for the Royal Palaces.

The workers of Redbrook Linen Mill, weaving tea towels, c. 1940's.

The sewing staff of William Sugden and Sons, Empire Mills, Stocks Lane, Barnsley. The premises pictured here were built in 1912, and were considered to be one of the most modern and well equipped factories in the Country. During the Second World War, the staff made over four million garments for the Forces.

William Sugden and Sons, Empire Mills, c. 1930's. The working conditions may have been considered first rate in those days, but by today's standards they look extremely cramped and the noise level must have been unbearable. No wonder not many of the women can manage a smile for the photographer.

The last working handloom weaver in Barnsley was Mr Robert Darling, pictured here working at Thomas Taylor and Son, in the early 1900s.

In 1790, Mr Edward Lancaster, a prominent local gentleman, laid the foundation stone for the firm of Lancasters. Over 200 years later the name of Lancasters is still well known to the people of Barnsley. The Lancaster family became involved in many aspects of the Town's life. Mr E G Lancaster, pictured here with members of his family, established the Church of St Edward the Confessor in Barnsley.

The Chemical Works at Wombwell, in the 1950's.

The Barnsley Brewery Company Ltd, as it was on 15 July 1957. The famous Oakwell brewery closed in February 1973, despite a three year battle to stop the closure. Officially launched in 1888, the Company owned no less than 93 licensed premises. The Company was a pioneer in the use of steam traction engines, which were used to make deliveries. Mr Guy Senior, one of the eight men who formed the Company, was called upon to defend the excessive speeds reached by these vehicles–often over 4 mph.

The dark and gloomy assembly shop of Jabez and Nall and Company Ltd, makers of crates. The Company was based at Springvale, Penistone.

No time for school, in the early 1900's. Young boys man the assembly line, hooping and wire binding at Jabez and Nall and Company Ltd.

Barnsley has always been well known for the number of its Public Houses. One of many was the Coach and Horses Commercial Hotel, on the corner of Peel Square and Market Hill.

The Old White Bear Inn, Shambles Street, pictured here shortly before demolition in 1954. The earliest known landlord was Mr Benjamin Strut, who was in residence from 1818 to 1835. However, the Old White Bear was in existence as early as 1717, as we know a dinner was held there during the Barnsley Races of that year. The Central Library, Barnsley now stands on the site of the Inn.

Closing time at the Norman Inn, Monk Bretton, *c.* 1900.

Monk Bretton Club, *c*. 1900. It is easy to see how important Working Men's Clubs have been over the years, the street on which the Monk Bretton Club stands is called Club Street.

The last part of the demolition of Clarkson's Brewery, 1980. The Old Brewery was founded in 1839. The Clarkson Public Houses were to be found within a small radius of Barnsley; none was outside the old West Riding boundaries. The brewery was acquired by Tennant Brothers of Sheffield in 1956. The brewery was closed shortly afterwards and subsequently demolished.

Happy to be at work? The employees of Roggins Quarry, Silkstone, stand proudly by their modern machinery.

Naylor Brothers (Clayware) Limited, Cawthorne. The business started in around 1840, as Naylor Roberts and Pearson, Contractors. This partnerships was dissolved in March 1860 and George William Naylor and his brother Thompson founded Naylor Brothers, railway contractors, at Cleckheaton in about 1870. The Clayworks were founded sometime around 1890–1900, using the clay deposits they discovered while working on a viaduct in Denby Dale. In 1948, the Cawthorne branch of the Naylor Brothers was established, as shown in the photograph.

The kiln at Milton Pottery, Hoyland.

Workmen repairing the 210 feet high chimney stack at Rylands Glass and Engineering Company. The Company was built in 1889, and described as 'the largest bottle and box manufacturers in the Kingdom, if not the World'.

Women on the production line at Ceag Ltd during the 1930s. Ceag Ltd came to the fore during the First World War. The Company became a well known name in mining circles. They were specialists in the design and manufacture of lamps for use underground. During the mid 1920's they entered the field of manufacture of bulbs for the motor industry. In 1935, the factory was completely destroyed by fire, but was rebuilt the following year.

The machine section of the Glass Bottle Makers of the Yorkshire United Trade Protection Society, Stairfoot Branch, pictured here in 1914. Mr J Ashworth, Vice President, and Mr H Eaton, President are seated centre of front row.

J.A. Porter, Fruiterer on Agnes Road –
Barnsley tradesmen in the late 1800s.

The wide selection of meats available at
Hunters.

Hirst's the family of butchers who brought us the Barnsley Chop (and some wonderful pork pies) began in this shop in Cheapside in 1897. Albert Hirst, the founder, had three sons who all followed him into the business. After the Second World War, their fame spread far and wide when Albert Hirst (the second) won the European Black Pudding Championships in France and was crowned Black Pudding King.

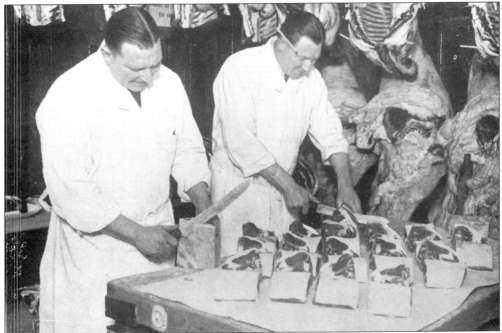

Mr Albert Hirst and his brother John are pictured here preparing the famous Barnsley Chop for HRH The Prince of Wales on the opening of Barnsley Town Hall 13th December 1933. The Barnsley Chop is famous throughout the world and can be found on the menu of New York's Waldorf Astoria Hotel.

Although Barnsley is known as an industrialised area, agriculture plays an important part in the local economy. September means harvest time for workers pictured here loading oats at Cawthorne, c. 1958.

'I don't think there's room for much more.'

Mr Jim Clegg, Robert and Harry Bottom (and tractor), Cawthorne 1958.

Mr Harry Bottom, Hay Swather, Cawthorne 1958.

Two farmers rest their legs at Cross Lane Hoylandswaine c. 1860's.

Five
The Best Days of
Our Lives

'Now get into pairs and form an orderly line'. The children of Lamb Lane Infants School, Monk Bretton, wrap up warm and look ready to go home.

Barnsley Girls High School, post 1905.

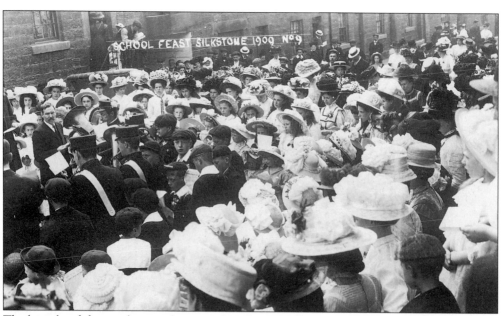

The brass band draws a large audience and a selection of wonderful bonnets at the school feast at Silkstone 1909.

The boys and girls of Crane Moor Infants School Wortley look less than pleased to be having their class photo of 1922 taken. The girls with ribbons in their hair, the boys with sailor style collars but not one with a smile. The school closed in July 1985.

The austere frontage of the Council Schools at Grimethorpe 1913.

Dressed in their Sunday Best, pupils and their families from the Mount Cerizim Methodist Chapel Sunday School are ready for their outing on a sunny morning in 1875.

The School Boards first school was opened on Snydal Lane, Cudworth in 1901 by Mr W. Maycock, Chairman of the first board. The opening of the school marked the progress of Cudworth from a quiet rural village into a busy centre.

Pupils wait for the gates of Royston Board School, Midland Road to open. The school was built in 1896 and demolished in 1988.

The pupils of Hunningley Lane Stairfoot turn out *en masse* for their photograph. The girls wear smock aprons, the boys smart white collars, knee length breeches and flat caps.

There was a sharp rise in the incidence of tuberculosis during the First World War particularly in heavily industrialised areas. Wombwell Open Air School was the country's first special school for the sufferers of TB and was opened by Sir George Newman, Chief Medical Officer of the Board of Education on June 2nd 1932. In this photograph the children, all sufferers of TB, a disease which could often prove fatal, await the arrival of their mid-day meal.

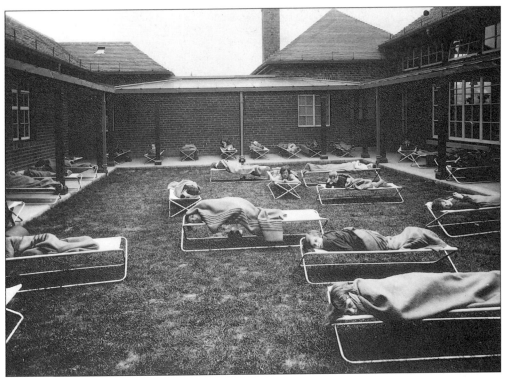

The children take a rest period in the open air.

The school which housed around 60 pupils was specially designed with large windows so that the children could sit in the fresh air.

Batons at the ready. The Great Houghton Church of England School Rounders Team of 1932 prepare to enter battle.

Kings Road School Wombwell was opened on September 2nd 1905 and described at the time by the West Riding County Council as the 'plum of the Riding'. The School, designed by Mr John Robinson, cost £10,087 4s 3d. to erect.

Crane Moor Sunday School outing *c*. 1950.

Staff at Doncaster Road School *c*. 1930.

The Lamb Lane Infants drinking their morning cup of milk.

'Open wide'. The Infants watch in eager anticipation as a dose of cod liver oil is administered to a classmate.

What is the woman in the white coat and bandage in hand doing to these children? The three children on the left have obviously been through the process, as the rest look nervously at the camera.

'Shine your shoes Sir?'

A less than appetising school dinner judging by the looks on the children's faces. Some things never change.

Physical exercise for the pupils of Athersley South Junior School, 1957.

The extremely well presented staff and pupils of the Mount Gerizim Primitive Methodist Chapel c. 1875. Wasp waists, lace collars, smocks and tie up boots were very much the fashion.

Class of 1954 – the pupils of Hoyle Mill County Primary School complete with saggy socks and smiles.

The Technical College on Church Street was officially opened by Alderman H.M. Walker J.P. on Monday October 10th 1932. This photograph was taken 31 years later in 1963.

Keir Street Junior School.

Artist at Work. The talented youngster featured here attended St. Matthew's Infants School, Summer Lane in the late 1960s.

'Hello Mum', Yvonne, Susan, Arthur and Derrick smile for the camera on a snowy day at St. Matthews in 1963.

Six

Getting Out and About
Transport in Barnsley

Barnsley Station on the North Midlands Railway line at Cudworth. This line was developed in 1836, with the aim of linking Derby and Leeds and opened for business in 1840. Stephenson refused to divert his railway into Barnsley and the people had to find other means of transport just to get to the railway station. The station was renamed Cudworth Station in 1854, after the Leeds and Manchester Railway and the South Yorkshire Railway opened their lines into Barnsley town centre.

Felkirk Church Bus in the 1950s. This bus was used to transport people to and from church throughout the surrounding areas.

Motorcycling memories. Albert and Hannah Hay and family set out from Redbrook Farmhouse.

Omnibus, Barnsley and District Electric Traction Company. The first Leyland 'subsidy' vehicles of this kind were introduced in August 1923. At the same time there were developments in the bus services in the Barnsley area. These were the introduction of the Barnsley to Thurnscoe via Wombwell, Wath, Bolton and Goldthorpe. It was not a coincidence that this route was developed at the same time that Thurnscoe constructed their own tramway system and that the new bus service followed the identical route of that taken by the trams.

Where's the fire? Inspector Weatherhogg and five volunteers on Churchfields, c. 1930.

A group of Barnsley men set off on their travels.

The Golden Age of Steam. Barnsley Courthouse Station looking east during the 1950s. The engine is probably the 'Cudworth Flyer'. Once the main lines were developed Cudworth and Barnsley somehow managed to get left behind. A diversion was built to serve Sheffield and the two coach shuttle train which followed became known as the Cudworth Flyer. The flyer made its final run in June 1958.

A later view of Barnsley Court House Station showing an example of a diesel locomotive on the line to Sheffield. The station was modernised in 1955 when it was given new canopies and lights. Needless to say the station was coming to the end of its days. The station was now only taking Barnsley – Sheffield traffic and some parcel trains. The station finally closed on April 5th 1960.

Monk Bretton Junction and Signal Box. The only stop between Barnsley and Cudworth, it closed in 1937.

Birdwell and Hoyland Common Station, 1911. The station almost looks like a miniature village compared to today's small station shelters.

Penistone Viaduct Crash February 1916. The accident occurred due to bad foundations under the viaduct which had progressively been worn away with rain and bad weather. The engine had to be cut into pieces before it could be removed – however they were still able to open the line in the very same year.

Cudworth Station, 1958 as the Cudworth Flyer enters the station at platform three. This was probably one of its last runs.

Penistone Old Station c. 1955. One would hardly expect Penistone to be a thriving railway centre. However, in the 1880s and 1890s it was exactly that, with a main line and two branch lines emanating from its five platform station. From Penistone you could travel to Sheffield, Manchester, Barnsley and Huddersfield (an essential station within the trans-Pennine line). In 1965, the passenger train service was threatened by re-organisation at Sheffield with a view to greater centralisation. The first closure was called off but inevitably the station was closed to passenger transport in 1970.

Cudworth Railway Accident January 1905. Three express trains were involved in this terrible accident in which six people were killed and over twenty injured.

Pratt's Garage on Pontefract Road, Cudworth *c.* 1925. 'Check the registration number and if it's had work done at Pratt's, it must be O.K.'

Queens Fruit and Vegetable Market *c.* 1913. With a horse and cart delivering goods. An unusual cart at that – it could almost be a hearse!

'Faster!, Faster!' Flooding at Lundwood.

Traction Engines at the Co-op Perseverance Estate. The engine delivered flour from the mill to the Co-op Shops. The engine was finally taken off the road in 1920.

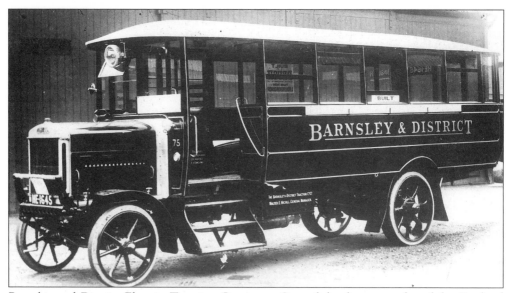

Barnsley and District Electric Traction Company. One of the first examples of the 'Leyland Subsidy' Vehicle.

Barnsley Bus garage and workers. Possibly one of the first buses built in 1926.

Runaway Tramcar Accident, December 2nd 1914. Seven people were injured in this accident. The double decker car, the property of the Barnsley and District Traction Company Limited, journeying between Smithies and Barnsley, got out of control and careered down Eldon Street North incline. Accounts state that as the tram arrived at Eldon Street Terminus the driver left his platform. During his absence the tram got into motion and gathered such a speed, that it jumped its rails. The tram came to a standstill by crashing into a general dealers shop owned by Mr J.C.Dodd.

Barnsley Bus Station opened in December 1938. Twelve thousand journeys per week were scheduled to depart from the new bus station. Contemporary reports described the bus station as one of the best in Yorkshire.

Barge moored on the canal at Barnsley. Note the alternative means of transport on board.

Dearne and Dove Canal at Worsborough 1954, looking down the eight Worsborough locks.

Beevor Hill Bridge Pontefract Road 1926. The building of the new bridge over the canal with the Barnsley Brewery in the background.

Upper Sheffield Road c. 1920 during the widening of the cutting. Note that there is little machinery evident for this type of work.

Joseph Locke – one of Barnsley's most famous sons. He was born in 1805 at Attercliffe in Sheffield and was responsible for the building of the Woodhead Tunnel which took six years to build at a cost of 28 lives. Locke died in 1860 and is buried in London. His statue which stands in Locke Park was designed and built by the Italian sculptor Marochetti after his death.

Elephants in Barnsley at the turn of the century. Although not a normal means of transport for Barnsley people, elephants are used as carriers and transporters in many parts of the world. These particular animals were part of a circus troupe although they appear to be doing a good job of carrying their trainer.

Seven
Around the Area

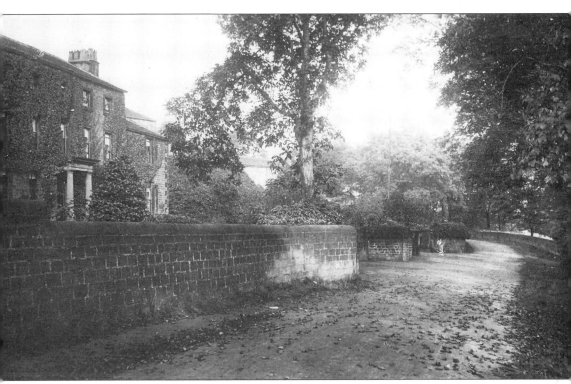

Ouslethwaite near Barnsley. Developed around 1760 this small village was at one time the home of the Elmhirst family – one half of the Barnsley solictors Elmhirst and Maxton.

A touch of the Orient *c.* 1900. The inhabitants of China Square, Crane Moor pose for the photographer.

Barrow Row. These houses were built for the first miners at Barrow Pit in 1875. They were built on Worsborough Park on the old road to Barrow.

Houghton Old Hall. The hall stood in the centre of the village of Great Houghton. Built probably in the latter part of the 16th century, it was for a long time the home of the Rodes family. Sir Edward Rodes served under Cromwell in the Civil War. In the early part of 1930 the hall narrowly escaped destruction by fire. The hall was demolished between 1959 and 1963.

Wentworth Castle, South Elevation, Stainborough in 1947. This photograph was taken prior to Captain Vernon Wentworth selling the house, the outbuildings and sixty acres of garden to Barnsley Education Committee. Death Watch Beetle, dry rot and military occupation caused considerable damage to the building, which the Wentworth family could not afford to repair. The house was therefore sold to the council and became a teacher training college in 1949. This institution was closed in the 1970s and the building was converted in 1978 to form the present day Northern College of Residential Adult Education.

Mr J. Silvester J.P., Chairman of Worsborough Urban District Council, cutting the first sod for the new council housing scheme, August 1920. The houses were built at Ward Green, specifically for the working classes and they were partly financed by the Ministry of Health. Sixty-two houses were built at a cost of just over £900 each. The event was attended by Sir James Hinchcliffe, Chairman of the West Riding of Yorkshire County Council and after the event, he and sixty other people had tea at the St. John's Ambulance room in Worsborough Bridge.

Mitchelson Avenue, Dodworth. Note the total absence of street furniture. For example there are no trees or even street lamps.

Towngate, Mapplewell with Greenside and Spark Lane at the top. The house in the centre was at one time a Police station.

High Street, Hoyland in the 1950s. This area has since been totally redeveloped. Note the sign for Oakwell Ales.

Market Street, Hoyland in the 1950s. The clock in the background was affectionately named 'Martha'.

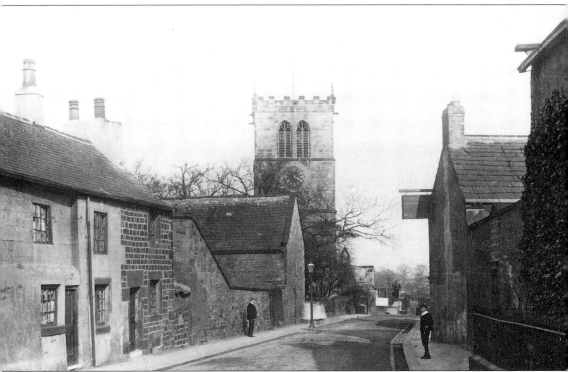

Halfway up Church Street in Darfield. The church is one of the oldest in the area and has in the graveyard a monument to the 149 men killed in a mine explosion at Lundhill Colliery 1857.

The River Dearne as it flows underneath the Saltersbrook Road at Darfield. Not far from this scene stood the old Toll house where the gate keeper used to live. In 1871, the gate, posts and toll boards were sold to Mr Heppenstall for £3 5s. The building eventually became a fish and chip shop.

The very chilly Cudworth open air swimming baths in the 1950s. The baths which were in the Welfare Park were covered and turned into an indoor complex during the 1960s.

The bandstand at Cudworth c. 1950. A very delightful and tranquil scene in which to enjoy concerts in the summer months.

The pond, Cudworth. This dry spot was once a real pond where people would skate in winter.

Hill Street, Elsecar c. 1950.

Elsecar by the sea. The park at Elsecar was a very popular place for people to go and relax. There was a refreshment room where you could get a cup of tea and a sandwich while the children played on the beach.

An idyllic rural scene at Skiers Hall, Elsecar, Low Wood. Skiers Hall was a building of ancient years. It passed through the hands of many families until it came into the ownership of the Earl Fitzwilliam in 1782. The hall was a tenement cottage until its demolition in 1951.

Elsecar Rifle Whist Drive, June 1911. This must have been a special event as all concerned are dressed in their Sunday best.

Village industry at Grimethorpe 1990.

In the shadow of the pit children play, Grimethorpe 1990.

A changing skyline, Grimethorpe 1990. The pit head, chimney and cooling tower have all now been demolished.

Grimethorpe High Street in the late 1800s. The town has gone through some incredible changes.

Lazy days in Church Street, Brierley. In 1869 George Savile Foljambe built Brierley Church, the spire of which can be seen in the background. Two years later the church school was built.

This photograph shows another part of Church Street in Brierley. This street was once the home of William Hanson's Smithy and the Three Horse Shoes Public House.

Coronation Bonfires. This was the bonfire lit at Stainborough.

The unveiling of the War Memorial at Cawthorne. The memorial was erected outside the museum and was unveiled on June 15th 1921 by Admiral Sir Henry Jackson.

Cawthorne Cross, 1908. This cross is situated in the village near the church of All Saints. Although called a cross it is actually a fountain. It was presented to the village by Miss Frances and Miss Maria Stanhope after a supply of water had been brought into the village in 1866.

Houghton Road, Thurnscoe *c*. 1950. An easy day to do some shopping.

Burton Abbey – almost certainly constructed by the monks at Bretton Priory.

Church Street, Darton *c.* 1950. Popplewell's hairdressers is still in Darton but the cottages at the bottom left are no longer in existence. The building where the telegraph pole stands is now the health centre.

The Isolation Hospital in Penistone *c.* 1905. Built at a cost of £6000 in 1904 from rock taken from Thurlstone and Shepley and situated at Hoyland Moor. The land was donated by Colonel Sir Walter Stanhope, and as a result it was called the Stanhope Isolation Hospital. The building was designed by Mr. G. Wilde and incorporated four hospital blocks; an eight bed scarlet fever block and four bed typhoid block; an adminstration block and the washing and drying block.

Market Street, Penistone looking north 1914.

Great snows at Penistone, February to March 1933. Gordon Heeley, the son of a Penistone cobbler, is shown here struggling through the snow in Penistone Market Street. The problems did not end with snow as heavy rains led to later flood alerts.

The River Dearne in flood, April 13th 1970.
Taken at Abbey Lane looking toward Grange
Lane. During this catastrophe, which had over
twenty-eight hours of rain, several houses
were flooded out.

Bridge Mill, Monk Bretton. An all too typical
scene of the demise of the industrial
revolution.

The Post Office at Monk Bretton *c.* 1900.

Monk Bretton Cross, High Street *c.* 1910.
This cross was once better known as Butler
Cross.

Wombwell High Street *c.* 1907. This postcard was addressed to Mrs Nickols of Wombwell House, Great Yarmouth. The message read 'Bird Arrived. That is my little girl at the front of Wilson's shop. G. Guest.'

Dearne Paper Mill fire in 1913. The Mill was owned by Messrs Marsden and Sons but the site became occupied by the Star Paper Mill which closed in 1981.

Noblethorpe Hall, Silkstone. An artist's impression made during the 1840s. This was the residence of J.S.H. Fullerton Squire of Silkstone. The old house, which was a manor residence similar to Woolley Manor, was purchased by James Clarke, an attorney and colliery owner. The house was rebuilt by Mr. Robert Cauldwell Clarke in 1838 who turned it into a stately mansion with large gardens and a pleasant park. In recent years the Hall has been left to ruin but the Hall has been sold to a new owner who intends to return it to former glory.

Acknowledgements

Thanks must go to the employees of the Barnsley Archive Service who compiled this book: Miss Louise Whitworth, Mrs Gillian Nixon and Mrs Carol Tague. Special thanks must be extended to Mr Maurice Hepworth, without whose great knowledge and patience we would on many occasions have been very bewildered by the whole project; to Mr Neil Randerson who helped with the research.

Acknowledgements for photographs to: Mr R. Portman, Mr Sid Jordan, William Sugden and Sons (Empire Mills), Mr E. Tasker, Sheffield Newspapers, Mr John Hislop, C.E.A.G., Mr John Nixon, Vicki Hoyland, Naylor Brothers, Mr Richard Morton, Mr Stephen McClarance, Mr Harry Brookes.

The Barnsley Archive Service would like to dedicate this book to Walt Swift whose love and knowledge of Barnsley and its history is missed by so many.